GasLit!

Mira

ISBN-13: 9798417458224
ISBN-10: 9798417458224

Cover design by: Art Painter
Library of Congress Control Number: 2018675309
Printed in the United States of America

This book is dedicated to everyone who has gone through abuse, to my children and family who have been my anchor and beacon of light through the dark days.

Contents

<h1 style="text-align:center">Preface</h1>

WHY THIS BOOK?

I have had several relationships; I was married to a physically abusive person, and my last relationship was with an someone emotionally abusive. Walking away from the physically abusive relationship was way easier even though we shared children. Why was it easier you may ask? The physical wounds, a black eye, swollen lip, bruises or handprints caused by slaps are easy for me to discern, explain and hard to hide. These wounds being visible was not difficult to describe and to justify your need to leave that relationship. Other people, friends, family, police including medical officers are more understanding, accept that you are being abused, will support and encourage your decision to protect yourself and your children from further abuse. Emotional and psychological abuse are harder to explain as there are no visible wounds, most times this form of abuse is regarded as a lesser injury. Mental abuse is not clearly visible, may take years and some people never realize that they are being abused or be able to articulate what they are going through. This form of abuse can be numbing. The black eye of soul, the bruises to one's self-esteem, cracked confidence, bumps to the mind are injuries that emotionally abused people have which can go on for years before one realizes the extent of damage done to them. Anytime one raises this form of injury to try and explain their situation, most people get uncomfortable discussing or are mostly ignorant of emotional abuse and want to refer one to mental health specialists pushing one further to self-doubt and exclusion. The stigma of any form of abuse is common but the stigma for emotional abuse is extremely damaging. mental abuse is even harder as the abuser is usually charming to the world and will usually claim to be the victim while you the abused are left ostracized. Your fight is usually your own for a very long time! Most of the war is in your mind. Walking away from this type of abuse is difficult as manipulation is hard to fight. It is a long painful lonely road of realization, survival and final decision to walk away or continue persevering. Unfortunately the damage of emotional abuse is felt by everyone you encounter, because this form of abuse changes your being making one to be moody, untrusting, shunning friends and family, reckless, less focused, prone to outbursts which makes one difficult to live or work with. Like, I said earlier its a long lonely road.

.

Prologue

Am I crazy?

Are you crazy?

Are we all crazy?

I love you; I hate you sometimes!

You are annoyed, spiteful, hateful!

Am stunned, infuriated, disgusted, livid!

Your words are unrecognizable, inhuman.

Did you just say that? Did you mean it?

You loved me yesterday, you hate me now.

Am happy, sad, cheery, pained, ecstatic, insane.

I was your true love earlier, worst enemy now,

You are my soulmate; Jackpot, I thought.........!

Have you felt like this in your life?

Ok, continue reading......

I love sad songs?

I love watching sad movies?

I feel taken for granted?

I dress, eat, walk, smile, talk, cook, socialize, for you!

This relationship is full of drama, a rollercoaster ride without a rest, maybe a little.

Everyone wonders that I am are still in this relationship?

I am exhausted, unfocused, moody, unmotivated, bored?

I fear that I could punch or even kill, but am afraid of jail?

This road seems familiar, I have been on this road before.

I thought my love was enough to change my soulmate?

Love must be the cure!

Sometimes I too question my sanity.

Friends and family just wonder why I do not leave or why I keep going back.

The Reveal

I will take you through the craziness maze....

Some people do not understand what is going on or that they are victims of emotional abuse, they are confused by their relationships.

I hope this will enlighten you....It may be triggering.

I am not a psychiatrist or claim any medical knowledge of what you or someone you know is going through. I am just putting pen to paper to share what I know personally and have gone through this journey of insanity and pain.

I hope to make you understand that you are not crazy, you are strong, you are being abused.

You must be kind, loving, understanding, forgiving, overly optimistic.

You have hope in humanity, ever trusting, enduring.

You care, too much most times.

Crazy.

The '*Miranda*' *of gaslighting* -
anything you say or do can and will be used against you in the court of the gas lighter. Your past hurts, secrets, your looks, your weight, failed previous relationships, family disagreements, illnesses, any private discussions about anyone will be used as ammunition when there is a disagreement. Nothing is sacred. Everything you shared in trust will be flung back to your face. The utter shock when the 'devil' reveals themselves, will take your breath away. The meanness, the lack of decorum, the shame that pours over you, the disgust that a human being albeit a close one, has no qualms in 'washing your dirty linen in public' or at your most vulnerable moment. You will be stunned! How can this be your soulmate, lover? This creature who is talking is not anyone I know. Physically yes, but the hate, the incredible meanness, the abject lack of empathy is something foreign, you do not know this evil monster. But alas, it is real, welcome to the land of gaslighting. You are gaslit!

Cuckoo.

You are walking on eggshells; you must be careful not to rock the boat. Do not ask questions in the morning … it is too early; do not ask questions in the evening it is too late. Make sure your tone is right, you are smiling. The food, your mood, your clothes, your time, what you watch, what you read is dictated by the gas lighter otherwise all hell will break loose. The trigger can be anything, a gesture, checking your cell phone, even receiving a call, your child interrupting a discussion. Once the trigger is pulled, the bomb of madness has exploded.

Madness.

Crazy bomb has exploded, argument starts, cups are flung, walls are punched, yelling, tirade of verbal abuse, a slap, a kick, a shove may happen. Your insecurities, fears, secrets are used against you. Keeping quiet does not make it better, it only makes them dig deeper into their hate sack; they will goad you incessantly, pulling out more hate, that sack has no depth! They will keep on until your patience runs out, your lid of anger explodes. Your own crazy rears its head and all reason may flee. You start spewing ugly words that you did not know you are capable of uttering. You may hit, throw or break something in return to reduce the pain. You just want the painful words to stop! They have succeeded in turning you to be a monster like them, even for a moment. They have gained more ammunition to use against you - you are the crazy one.

The devil smiles.

You hate what you are becoming!

After the blast.

The blast is over, time to clear the debris.
The windows to your soul broken,
The doors to your heart were torn apart
The roof of your brain was ripped out.
The taps of love are broken and dry now.
You are stunned, looking at what was.
Your hope in bliss, now shredded to bits!
You look around at the remainder of your life.
Uneasy calm settles.
Maybe someone walked away,
Or someone got into a drunken stupor, maybe an intervention by someone the gas-lighter respects.
Your shaken being comes to the realization that you really do not understand anything anymore.
You don't know this person!
It's happening again!
Am I crazy, are you crazy, did that really happen, did you say those words, did I say those words, did you mean them, do you hate me that much, am I that useless?
If it is the first time, you will be hurt beyond measure.
If you stay, this is played on repeat mode with increasing crescendo of hurtful words, more physical abuse, until you are numb to the pain, used to the hateful words, getting a little to being a monster too. I hate it here, you say!

Toothpaste Can't Go Back in the Tube.

For you, hate filled words cut deeper than anything you have experienced. Your self-esteem is dealt a blow, you become fearful, confused, indecisive! Your whole world is shrinking due to your pain, wanting to hide from the world. To minimize the pain, you may turn to booze, drugs, food, gambling or religion, anything to numb the pain. The worst is yet to come. Your hurt will be minimalized, your pain trivialized. You are told that you misunderstood the words - I did not say those words! You are too sensitive; you are making up stories. You are crazy, everyone knows you are! No wonder no one wants you. Remember it will all be your mistake, you caused all this to happen, you are the problem. Gaslighting at its best!

Take you to the moon.

Taken to the moon you thought, yes this felt real, this was your soulmate. In the beginning it will feel that way. I promise you it will feel like you landed on the moon. you gush with happiness, with awe, the ethereal feeling.
Never felt this love, you tell yourself, lol.
Soon the moon is dark, feels cold, lonely, rocky, non-productive. You look at the world from afar. You are isolated. No friends, no family, the worst of the abused may be told to quit their job or business. You are literally 'on the moon' going around the earth -, a constant, cyclical, cold, dark, boring, unexciting lonely life. Your world literally shrunk.

Jealous triangles .

If you thought that was all, no darling. Another tool in the gas lighter's sack is pulling you into discussions about another person to throw you off balance. They will tell you how someone else is interested in them, might show you communications or pictures of other people, some real or imaginary, and compare you to others, even celebrities. Pitting you against relatives, friends and even children is their *modus operandi*, This is all done to make you feel hurt, insecure, jealous, bitter, confused and all for what gain, so that you cause drama. They feed their ego on drama. They are drama vampires who flourish when you exhibit jealousy, it makes them invincible. On the flip side it gives them more ammunition to call you crazy and unstable. They want to break you and then tell you that you are jealous and have low self-esteem. For children in your life, they are pawns, they may lavish love and gifts to their perceived favorite, making the others feel unloved and causing a lot of friction between siblings. Divide and rule is their game and they do not care about the long-term relationship damage they cause these unsuspecting children.

Flying monkeys.

The gas lighter is very charming and pleasant in public, their real persona is hidden. Tarnishing your name is a very useful tool of the gas lighter to isolate you. They do this by having loyal people – flying monkeys who have been fed lies to mark you as a flawed person:- who is a drama queen, crazy, unstable, may be called a drunk. These may be friends, relatives, children or even religious leaders. The flying monkeys may not be hostile to you but know that they do not have your interests at heart, most likely everything you say about the abuser is reported back to them. All complaints about how you are being treated by the abuser are treated with disdain and words like 'they did not mean it', 'you are overreacting', 'maybe you did something to annoy them", "but they love you", "you are ungrateful", "they provide for you ". All this is to shield the abuser from blame. While the flying monkeys may not be aware that they are abetting abuse, they make it harder for you to seek help or trust anyone, further making your isolation more real and traumatic. Depression, destructive modes of coping become prominent in your life. You may find yourself engaging more in substance abuse like alcohol, drugs, pornography, gambling, eating disorders and many other unhealthy habits.

Sleep deprivation.

Normal people need a good night's sleep to function the next day. Gas lighters use sleep deprivation as a tool to destabilize you. Just like criminal interrogation tactics use lack of sleep to break criminals. It will be used on you to elicit anger or to enhance their fragile ego, by asking you to get them food in the wee hours of the night, They may make startling noises like playing music too loud, doors being banged or shut loudly, asking you to listen to their day's/night's experiences just for the heck of it. Show your anger or lack of interest at their waking you up and hell has no bounds, you may just have triggered the crazy bomb. That will be the end of a peaceful night for you. They have won again by depriving you of sleep. This may make you cranky, susceptible to outbursts and being less productive the next day. This method just worsens your days and darkens your soul. The abuser is slowly winning in diminishing you, draining your energy, mental acuity by making you tired from lack of sleep. You are slowly fading!

Children - golden & scapegoat.

This is the worst topic in the gaslit story because it affects an innocent soul, one, who does not deserve this bullshit. Like I stated, gas lighters have no limits in their deranged ways to gaslight you. They do not care for anyone else other than their overblown ego. Children are collateral damage in most situations. They will pit children against you, against each other all for their own benefit. Some children may be elevated as their favorites - golden child, may be used to spy on you, to make them look good, to make the other children jealous. The unfortunate children are ridiculed and gaslighted like you - the scapegoat.
Lo, if it is a blended family, they will show shameless favoritism to their own or on other occasions all the children are gaslighted. The abuse of the children is usually the breaking point that leads you away- a bridge too far!

No Soul.

Emotional abusers are incapable of feeling anyone's pain, they lack empathy. Your pain, your loss, your defeat even death or sickness in your family, is an inconvenience to their comfort. You have no right to be sad or unhappy. You want to cry; you are spoiling the mood, its death; accept it; God comes for his people, nothing to comfort you. Do not dare cry, ultimate crime! You are weak! Get over it already. Personal testimony, my best friend was shot and died, I had to hold my tears until the gas lighter was not in the house to cry. I had to hide my pain while I was grieving only allowing myself to mourn when alone, crying in the car driving to work. It may come as a shock to know that abusers want you for themselves and are extremely jealous and insecure, though you are always labeled the insecure jealous one. Friends and relatives in their twisted minds are a threat and so mourning them is an act of disloyalty. Remember, isolation is a powerful tool in a gaslighters sack.

Is this all?

NOPE!

Emotional abuse is vast and you need to educate yourself further. Like I said, I do not have any medical certifications to diagnose mental health abuse. To understand and make sense of what I was going through, I started writing this book. I started reading and buying books to learn the different personalty disorder that make a seemingly normal person can morph into a monster whose words and actions did have a profound effect on my life and changed me in ways that are still unraveling.

TIPS!

Learn about your abuse.

Acknowledge abuse

If still in the relationship learn the triggers and work around them.

Learn 'gray rocking" if safe, become uninteresting and unresponsive to the the goading, walk away - again if safe. Bite your tongue, do not respond.

Plan your exit, emotional abusers never change, only change tactics and methods of manipulation.

"No matter how much a snake sheds the skin. It's still a snake"
~ Unknown

Financial abuse.

What is financial abuse? It is controlling a victim's ability to acquire, use, and maintain financial resources. This is perhaps one of the most powerful methods of keeping a victim trapped in an abusive relationship. The gas lighter might manage all the finances and monitor all your financial transactions. In some relationships they may make you totally dependent on them by refusing you to have a source of income. The often ignored part of financial abuse is the hands off, having a partner who just sits and watches movies, playing video games and does not contribute in the financial upkeep of the family. They may completely decline in contributing to the household finances, may refuse to work, which means you have to work full time and for low wage earning victims, this may mean working two or three jobs to pay bills. This ensures that you are bone tired, your immune system is lowered and mentally exhausted, making you susceptible to opportunistic diseases, emotional outbursts or you may develop negative methods of coping, this pushes the narrative that you are mentally unstable. crazy!

To me.

Am I: -

This naïve?

Such a weakling?

Just scared to be lonely.

Afraid of walking away?

In love with getting hurt.

Holding on for me or for my children?

Saving face? Everyone told me it was a bad idea.

Do I enjoy the , the craziness, the insensitivity, ingratitude?

Deep down I know I deserve better. I do not like this!

To you.

Do not think I do not know!

Do not think that for one minute I forgot my pain.

Do not think with your smooth talk, I do not remember.

Do not think that I am a fool to think you will change.

Do not think that your smile still gives me illusions.

Your words are losing the sting that broke me before.

I know you are the problem.

I know I am not crazy, unstable, useless, jealous.

I know that I am strong, beautiful and wiser.

I will rise again!

I will love again and be loved equally!

I deserve better! I deserve the best! I deserve peace at least!

It will be hard I know to shake the talons of the pain and fear you have instilled in my heart, my mind and my soul.

I getting wiser and surely I will triumph, even if I must limp or crawl to the finish line.

I am building a moat around my castle!

A moat to protect the castle of my heart, mind, and life.

I will live in this castle where your spears of hateful words and actions will not pierce my heart, will no longer hurt!

Your roar of hate will not shake my castle or shock me into numbness, because I now know the dark side of your beautiful smile, the depths of your evilness.

I will smile, I will sing, I will dance, I will laugh.

Yes, I will prevail.

I refuse you to soil my castle of self-love and preservation with your poison.

I refuse you to control me, my mood, my mission, my vision, my happiness, my joy.

All because I realized I had given you the power to drive me crazy, the control knobs to my emotions.

I have taken back the steering wheel and in hands have the knobs to still me.
I will not be mad, yell, no longer will I beg for your love, respect or understanding.

I am getting stronger, I will take control of my life, my future and most importantly my happiness.

I am in control of my life's rudder, the heights I will scale and the lows I will deep.

You do not have that control anymore. It's mine!

I am strong, I am good, I am wonderfully made, I am an individual like no other and I do not seek to ape another.

I am a normal person, I am not crazy, and I deserve better.

Deserve and desire.

I deserve happiness, security, a faithful partner.

A partner who will share joy, happiness, the beauty of this world, life's curve balls.

A soulmate who shares a vision of a beautiful life, my ambitions.

A trusted friend, who truly has my back, who will not abuse my trust weather in deed or word.

Someone I can respect, love, trust, feel free without a care.

A real person with a soul and a heart that beats and feels genuinely for another human being.

I will bring my imperfections and together we will try smooth my rough edges to create an imperfect beautiful union.

A human not perfect but a person with a Soul!

So, what now?

If any of this has resonated with you, know that you are being abused and you may need counseling. You will hear about narcissists, covert and overt ,sociopaths, psychopaths etc., Arm yourself with knowledge. There are many resources online that will help. If you are not ready to go to counseling, spend time learning about your abuse and how to overcome this form of abuse without getting hurt. The most important thing is acknowledging that there is a problem in your relationship. This abuse may be from your parents, intimate partner, siblings, relatives or your own children, even co-workers. I do recommend reading books or free online resources on narcissitic, emotional and mental abuse. Learn self-care - a walk in the neighborhood alone, reading self improvement books, reconnecting with friends or trying to make new friends, declutter and clean your living enviroment, this has a positive effect of clearing your mind too. Do a financial review and plan. Have a hairdo, manicure, pedicure, eyebrows. Small changes have a great impact on healing and regaining self confidence.

Remember: -

"Rest and self care are so important. When you take time to replenish your spirit, it allows you to serve others from the overflow. You cannot serve from an empty vessel".

~ Eleanor Brownn

Afterword

If a person can love you unconditionally, then that person can hate you unbelievably also!

Because:

"A beautiful mirror can turn into a dangerous weapon when broken."

~ Unknown

www.ingramcontent.com/pod-product-compliance
Lightning Source LLC
Chambersburg PA
CBHW071245140726
47996CB00007B/2765